Kids Gone Paddlin'

The Young Paddler's Guide to Having More Fun Outdoors

Tom Watson

Creative Publishing
international

About the Author

Tom Watson reviews and field-tests watercraft, camping and survival products. He spent 5 years as a Kodiak Island Search-and-Rescue member and more than 12 years as a guide and outfitter in Alaska. Tom is also the author of *How to Think Like Survivor*. He lives in Owatonna, MN.

To Angelique, always adventurous, always loving!
May you always be a kid at heart!

Creative Publishing international

Copyright © 2008 by Creative Publishing international, Inc.
Creative Publishing international, Inc.
400 First Avenue North
Suite 300
Minneapolis, MN 55401
1-800-328-3895
www.creativepub.com
All rights reserved.

KIDS GONE PADDLIN'
by Tom Watson
President/CEO: Ken Fund
Publisher: Bryan Trandem
VP Sales & Marketing: Peter Ackroyd
Acquisition Editor: Barbara Harold
Creative Director: Michele Lanci-Altomare
Senior Design Manager: Brad Springer
Design Managers: Jon Simpson, Sarah Holle
Production Managers: Laura Hokkanen, Linda Halls
Cover Design: Wendy R. Lutge
Page Layout: Wendy R. Lutge
Illustrator: Tom Wallerick/Genesis Design Lab

All Photographs © Tom Watson, except: © Lili Colby: p. 25; © Lena Conlan: p. 27, 33, 34 (both), 58 (top), 70–71, 73, 75, 78–79, 82–83, 86–87, back cover (bottom); © Istock Photo: p. 7, 11, 14, 15, 16, 36, 43, 51, 54—55, 58 (bottom), 62, 64–65, 66, 80–81, 84, 85, back cover (middle right); © Tom Migdalski: front cover, p. 48; © David Nord: p.19, 31, 39, 52–53; © One Ocean Kayaks: p. 20, 21 (all); © Michael Powers: p. 24; © SealLine: p. 56, 57 (bottom); © J. Taylor: p. 5

Printed in China
10 9 8 7 6 5 4 3 2 1

Library of Congress Cataloging-in-Publication Data
Watson, Tom
  Kids gone paddlin' : the young paddler's guide to having more fun
outdoors / Tom Watson.
     p. cm.
  ISBN-13: 978-1-58923-371-3 (soft cover)
   ISBN-10: 1-58923-371-9 (soft cover)
  1. Boating for children. 2. Water sports. I. Title.
  GV777.56W38 2008
   797.1083--dc22   2007033515

Gone Paddlin' Message

If you're like most kids who love the outdoors, you want to do more than go on picnics or hike a nature trail. You want to go on the WATER. You want to paddle a boat.

By reading *Kids Gone Paddlin'*, you'll learn how. You'll find GREAT TIPS for choosing the best watercraft, paddles and gear. You'll even find ideas for other things to do.

It might take you a while to read this book, because it is filled with ideas for THINGS TO DO. You might stop reading right in the middle of a page, to go out and try a new skill. And that's great, because the better you get at those skills, the more fun you'll have on your next water adventure.

So read the tips, practice at home before you go, and then head for the great outdoors.

Happy PADDLING!

Contents

Canoe or Kayak?

Humans have been traveling on rivers and lakes for thousands of years. People learned to make boats from the materials around them. They built boats to hunt and gather food. They used the boat like we use a car to carry people from one place to another. Handmade boats helped early people live from the sea.

Today, we use the same kind of boats—canoes and kayaks—to play on the water. We fish and watch wildlife from them, or we take journeys down rivers, through country with lots of lakes, and even across oceans.

CANOES

The first canoes were made from carved-out tree trunks and called dug-out canoes. Many of the different kinds of canoes we use today are like the "skin" boats built by the first inhabitants of the North Pacific area. They used skins of animals to cover a frame made from trees and animal bones.

American Indians built boats using the bark from a birch tree. The bark tears off the trunk in sheets and can be used to cover the frame. Thread made from the roots of spruce trees or from animal intestines was used to help sew the bark together. Sap from trees was made into a waterproof glue.

Today, strips of wood from cedar and ash trees are popular for making "strip" canoes. Canoes can also be built from man-made materials such as aluminum, plastic, fiberglass and graphite. They come in many different colors.

PARTS OF A CANOE

The front is called the bow. The back is called the stern. The center of the boat is called the midsection.

The edge or rim around the top of the canoe is called the gunwale (pronounced "gunnel"). The long pieces that stretch across the canoe are thwarts. Both the gunwale and thwarts help the canoe keep its shape and add strength.

Some canoes have a special thwart in the middle of the canoe called a yoke. The yoke has a shallow "U" formed into it. Where lakes and rivers are separated by short sections of land, you must carry your canoe from one body of water, over the land, to the other water close by. This is called a portage. The yoke fits around your neck

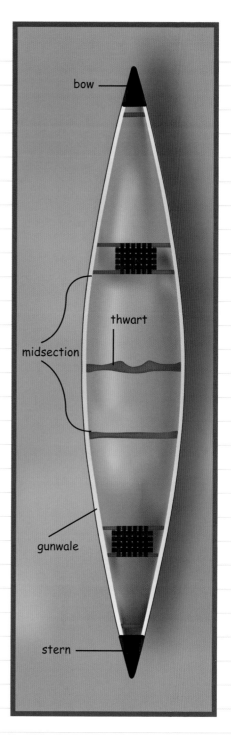

and lets you more easily carry most of the canoe weight on your shoulders.

Many canoes have bench-like seats covered in webbing. Others have a seat that looks like the seat on a tractor. It is molded to fit the shape of your rear end. Some people like the molded seat because it is more comfortable. It also helps you sit straight forward to paddle.

rocker

keel

The ends of the canoe are called stems. The higher the stem usually means a drier ride because it protects you from the water splashing up over the bow or stern. If you want to know how deep a canoe is, you measure it from the middle of the canoe.

The center line along the length of the bottom of the canoe is called the keel. It runs all along the boat from the bow to the stern. If you place a canoe on flat ground, it may lie flat all along the keel or it may curve up away from the ground at each end. That curve is called rocker.

A canoe with a flat keel is designed to go straight. Canoes that go straight without much effort are said to "track" well. These canoes are best used on open water where long, straight distances are paddled. Canoes with rocker are most often used on rivers where there are lots of turns to make and many obstacles to avoid. A canoe with rocker can turn more quickly and be maneuvered more easily. A canoe used in rapids and on very fast, whitewater of a river has a lot of rocker.

stem

SIZE AND SHAPE

The average length of a canoe is about 16 feet (14.9 m).

Most canoes are between 30 and 36 inches (76 and 91 cm) wide depending on how long they are.

Canoes made of aluminum and some plastics can weigh more than 60 pounds (27 kg). New materials are being used to make canoes that are the same size but much lighter. Some weigh less than 40 pounds (18 kg)!

16 feet

36 inches

The cross-section of some canoes at the widest part have flat bottoms; others are slightly "V" shaped. The flat bottom makes a very stable boat that can carry a lot of gear. A canoe with a slightly arched bottom can actually be more stable. As it carries more weight, the part of the boat down in the water becomes wider and makes the boat more stable.

TYPES & USES

Canoes used on rivers are often shorter than those used on the open water of lakes. Sometimes very tight turns are needed to go around bends in the river or to avoid rocks and trees in the water. A short canoe can turn quicker and easier than a longer canoe.

Specially designed canoes are used for racing down rivers, across lakes or over great distances on the ocean. A racing canoe can be very tippy.

Wide boats are usually more stable. Because they are usually shorter, they turn better than narrow boats, but they are harder to keep straight.

Some boats are built for just one paddler. The sides on these "solo" canoes are usually turned in so the boat is narrower where the paddler sits. This is called tumblehome, making it so the paddler doesn't have to reach out as far to paddle correctly.

Most canoes are designed to carry two paddlers. Longer canoes can usually carry a third person instead of extra gear. Some boats that are designed for one person can also be paddled by two smaller paddlers. There are some smaller "two person" canoes that can be easily paddled by one larger paddler.

If you want to carry a lot of gear, a longer canoe is better than a wider one because it will usually track better, too.

KAYAKS

A kayak is very similar to a canoe in many ways. It, too, comes to a point at the front and the back and is moved through the water by one or two paddlers. Kayaks come in a variety of shapes and lengths. Like canoes, they are designed to perform in special ways on the water.

deck

cockpit

bow

lines

coaming

stern

PARTS OF A KAYAK

Some parts of the kayak and canoe have the same names: the front of the boat is called the bow, the rear is called the stern. The center line down the middle of the bottom of the boat is called the keel. What makes each boat special are the differences between them.

A kayak has a deck that covers the top of the boat. In the center of the deck is a hole. This is called the cockpit. It is where the paddler sits. The special cover for this cockpit is called a spray skirt. It fits snugly around the waist of the paddler and then attaches to the rim of the cockpit (called the coaming). The spray skirt keeps water from getting inside the kayak. This keeps the boat dry and lets the paddler use the kayak even when the water is rough and washing up over the deck of the boat.

The deck has special lines attached to it. These are lengths of cord attached to the boat to help hold things on deck. Because the deck can be very slippery when wet, lines also help a paddler hold onto the kayak from the water.

forward hatch | bulkhead | cockpit | aft hatch | bulkhead

forward compartment | foot pedals | aft compartment

Because a kayak is covered by a deck, there is dry space inside the boat to carry gear and personal belongings. To reach inside the boat, kayaks have openings on the deck called hatches. The hatch has a waterproof cover so the inside stays dry.

The area inside the hatch is called a compartment. The compartment is separated from the rest of the inside of the boat by a wall called a bulkhead. The compartment in the front of the kayak is called the forward compartment. The one behind the cockpit is called the aft compartment.

A kayak usually has a handle near the bow and the stern of the deck. This handle makes it easier to carry the kayak to and from the water.

Many kayaks have either a rudder or a skeg to help keep the boat on course. A rudder swings back and forth and is moved using foot pedals inside the cockpit. A skeg is like a rudder blade except it only moves up and down, not side to side like a rudder. It is used to help the boat stay on a straight path through the water. The paddler can use a cable to lower the skeg down or to pull it back up.

down
position

up position

MATERIALS

Most kayaks are formed in molds that use either heated plastic or layers of glued fabric to give the boat its shape and strength. Boats made of heated plastic are baked in a big oven. When they cool and are "popped" out of the mold they are a complete, one-piece kayak.

Many kayaks are formed by adding layers of fabric that are soaked with a special glue, called resin. The material used to build these kayaks can be fiberglass or other lightweight, high-strength fabrics. Kayaks built using several different materials are called composite kayaks. The deck and the hull, or bottom, of the kayak are made as two pieces that are glued together. The boat is finished by adding all the different deck fittings and accessories.

The molded kayaks are heavier than the composite kayaks. Composite kayaks are more expensive than the plastic boats. Both types come in many different colors.

SIZE AND SHAPE

Whitewater kayaks are the shortest boats, some are only about 5 feet (1.5 m) long. A kayak for one paddler is usually 16 feet (5 m) long and about 22 inches (56 cm) wide. Some kayaks made especially for ocean surfing are more than 20 feet (6 m) long.

Kayaks are usually very narrow. Even longer boats that can carry three people are rarely wider than 30 inches (76 cm). A long kayak sometimes has a center cockpit for a third passenger.

Like canoes, the longer the kayak, the easier it is to track. Shorter kayaks are easier to maneuver. Kayaks are usually more stable as they get wider. Some kayaks of the same length can carry more gear than others because the body of the kayak is deeper. There is more distance between the center of the deck and the bottom at the keel. These are called high-volume kayaks.

16 feet

22 inches

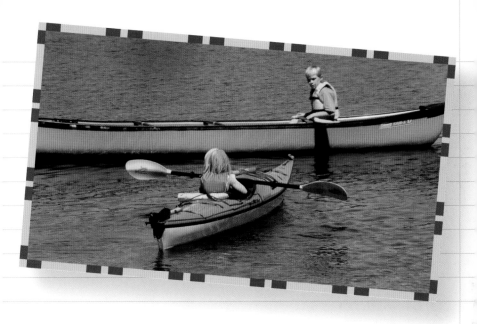

In a canoe, the paddler can move around a lot, face different directions and sit in different positions. In a kayak, the paddler has more contact with the boat. Good kayakers learn many ways to maneuver the kayak by leaning their body and sweeping with the paddle. A kayak is said to be "responsive" if it can be maneuvered easily.

A canoe can carry lots of gear because there is no top on the hull. A kayak has less room and usually carries less gear.

When placed side-by-side, a 16-foot (4.9 m) kayak is usually much narrower than a 16-foot (4.9 m) canoe. Because a kayak has a covered deck and sits lower in the water, it is usually easier to handle in rougher, windier weather than a canoe.

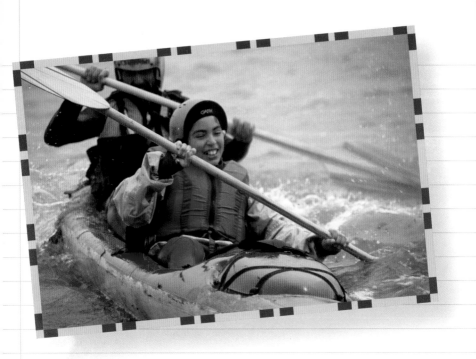

TYPES AND USES

Like canoes, kayaks that are shorter and wider are more stable. Most paddlers like to use them on calm and smooth water for fishing, photography and relaxed paddling. They can be easy to maneuver but don't go as straight or paddle as easily as the longer, narrower kayaks.

Shorter kayaks that have bigger cockpits are called recreational kayaks. They are used more for playing in the water and not meant for long trips.

Longer, narrower kayaks that are used for taking trips on the ocean or across big lakes are called touring kayaks. They can hold a lot of gear. They usually track (go straight) better. They move fast through the water and with practice are easy to steer and control.

A popular type of kayak is the whitewater boat. This is the short, stubby boat you may see in rapids on a river. These boats are specially designed for paddling in very wild and crazy water. There are also canoes that are especially designed for paddling in whitewater, too.

Another kind of kayak looks like a fat surfboard. It is called a Sit-On-Top kayak (SOT). The paddler sits on the kayak instead of inside it. Because they are very stable and comfortable for beginning paddlers these kayaks are very popular for fishing.

What Gear Do I Need?

If you enjoy spending time on the water, your most important piece of equipment is your life jacket, or PFD. That stands for Personal Flotation Device because they are made to keep a person floating in the water. Even if you are a good swimmer, you should always wear a PFD when in a boat.

Depending on where and when you go paddling, you may wear special clothing and take other gear. Of course, you will need paddles, too!

LIFE JACKETS

Type I

Type II

Type III

A life jacket will keep you afloat if you get separated from your boat. It should be colorful so you can be seen easily in the water. It must fit well to work well, so get the right one for you. Be sure you and your boating partners always wear a life jacket!

TYPES

Life jackets come in several different types. The PDFs used by canoers and kayakers is called a Type III. It is designed to hold your head out of the water.

Type I and Type II will actually turn you around so you float face up, even when you are unconscious.

The jackets used by canoers and kayakers are compact. They need to be small and comfortable so the paddler can easily move around.

PROPER FIT

Besides being the right size and type, a good life jacket must fit well. If it's too tight, it won't be comfortable, and if it moves around, it may not keep you afloat properly. Adult jackets are usually sized in inches; kids' jackets are sized by age.

The easiest way to see if the life jacket fits properly is to put it on and pretend you are paddling your boat. Sit on the ground and pretend you have a paddle and are sitting in your canoe or kayak paddling across a lake or river. Does the jacket give you enough room to move around and reach out for different parts of your make-believe boat? Does it pinch or poke you anywhere? Is it uncomfortable at all? If there is anything that doesn't feel right about your life jacket, you may not want to wear it.

MATERIAL

It's important to get a life jacket that is made out of good-quality materials that will last a long time. A good life jacket fits next to your body. A poorly fitting life jacket will shift around a lot.

SAFETY

Life jackets used for canoeing are usually basic and often don't have all the "extras" found on a kayaking life jacket.

The extras on a kayaking life jacket include several pockets and straps and loops so you can carry different types of small gear. Some of the items you might like to carry with you are a compass, a signaling whistle, a knife, maybe some snacks, too. Be careful not to fill the pockets so full that they start to bulge out.

Gear hanging on the jacket, as well as over-filled pockets, can get caught on lines, coaming and other parts of the deck. This can make it very hard or tiring to get back into the boat if you capsize.

Another important safety feature is the color of your life jacket. If you get separated from your boat, the color of your life jacket could help searchers find you.

Good colors for life jackets are bright yellow or orange, bright lime green and robin's-egg blue. Red may be an exciting color for racing cars and fire engines but it is not the best color for a PFD. It is hard to see at great distances, when it's really cloudy, or when the sun is low in the sky.

Another very important part of a good life jacket is a strip or patch of reflective tape. This tape reflects the light from a flashlight or spotlight and makes you easy to be seen even when it's too dark to see the entire boat.

Some life jackets have reflective patches on the panels in front and back and up on the top of the shoulder straps. If you have a life jacket that doesn't have reflective patches or stripes, you can buy reflective material in most marine hardware stores. It has sticky backing on it to let you put it anywhere you want on your jacket.

The most important safety tip about any kind of boating is to always wear your life jacket!

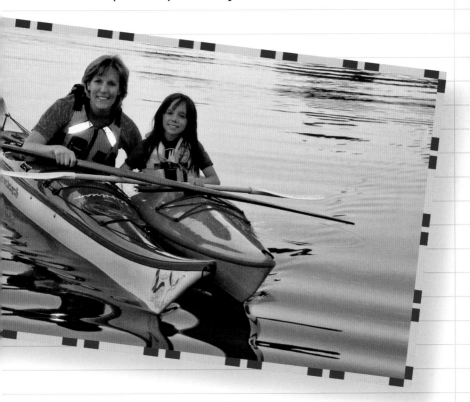

CLOTHING & ACCESSORIES

In general, you should wear clothing that is comfortable and quick drying. Be sure you know what the weather will be like when you go paddling. If it will be hot and sunny, you will want to protect your skin. If it will be cool, you will want to wear warmer clothing.

JACKETS, PANTS & BOOTS

If you paddle in cold water, you may want to wear a paddling jacket. It protects you from spray, from waves splashing against the boat and even from water dripping off the paddle. Most paddling jackets have hoods, collars, cuffs and waistbands that help keep water from getting inside your jacket.

Waterproof pants keep your bottom dry. Most of the time you can wear regular rain pants while paddling, especially when the water's cold.

Many paddlers don't wear shoes or boots at all. If you will be walking around in the water or on land, you might want some protection for your feet. Be sure you can still work the kayak rudder pedals.

HATS & GLOVES

A lot of body heat is lost through the top of your head. Even if you don't like wearing a cap or a hat, you should bring one with you in case of sudden changes in the weather.

Hats for paddling are just like any other hats for the outdoors. They keep you warm, or cool, or dry. A good option is to wear a wide-brimmed hat with a flap on the back to cover your neck from the sun.

If your hands get wet while you are paddling, they can get cold very fast. Most paddlers carry gloves with them, even on warm summer days.

Another good piece of equipment to keep hands dry and warm is called a pogey. It is like a mitten for the paddle! It is attached to the paddle and has an opening at the wrist so you can push your hand into the pogey to grab the paddle shaft.

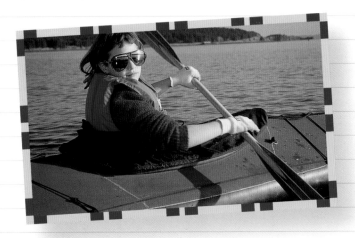

Other Gear

HERE IS A LIST OF THINGS YOU MIGHT WANT TO BRING ALONG ON ANY PADDLING TRIP:

Sunglasses — The polarized type is best, so you can see through the glare on the surface of the water

Nose plugs — You never know when you might capsize

Sunscreen — Sun reflecting off the water can give you a bad burn

Extra batteries — Carry different sizes

Binoculars — Great for wildlife watching

Compass and charts — Carry them in waterproof cases

Cell phone — Remember that some wilderness areas do not have service

Flashlight — Be sure it is waterproof

Extra matches — Campfires are easier to start

Signaling whistle — It makes a very shrill sound to attract attention

Boating knife — The wavy teeth on the cutting edge can be used to cut through rope

Throw line — It can be tossed to a paddler in trouble

Bilge pump — Kayakers carry this small hand pump to remove water from their boat

Deck sponge — Good for wiping water, sand and dirt off your seat

Bailing bucket — Canoers often tie a bailing bucket onto one of the thwarts

Dry bags — They protect everything from getting wet

PADDLES

You are the motor of your canoe or kayak. The paddle is like the propeller on an airplane. It makes the boat move forward or backward—even sideways! You use a paddle to move in all those directions, plus steer the boat. You also use it like a brake to stop the boat, or sometimes just to keep your balance on the water.

A paddle shaft is like your arm; the blade is like your hand. The blade of many paddles, especially those used for kayaking, is slightly curved— just like your hand while you are swimming.

PARTS OF A PADDLE

There are many things to consider when choosing the right paddle.

A canoe is usually paddled with just one blade. The blade is attached to one end of a short shaft. The other end is called the grip. It is where you grab the paddle to control the boat. Some solo canoers use a double "kayak" paddle with their canoes.

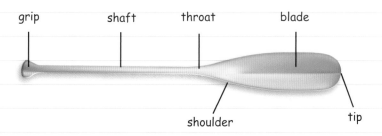

grip   shaft   throat   blade

shoulder   tip

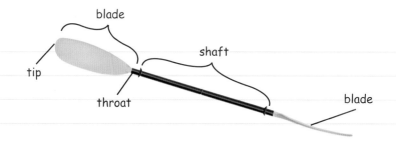

blade

tip

shaft

throat

blade

Kayak paddles have two blades at opposite ends of a long shaft. The outer end of the blade is called the tip, the part that connects to the shaft is called the throat. The side of the blade that faces the paddler and is used to pull water is called the power face. Usually a double paddle, such as those used for kayaking, has flattened sections on the shaft. This is where the paddler grips the shaft and controls the paddle.

Kayak paddles come in one-piece or two-piece types. One advantage of a two-piece paddle is that you can take it apart for storage on your boat or at home.

PADDLE LENGTH

Canoe paddles are usually measured in inches. The average paddle is between 52 and 56 inches (132-142 cm) long.

Most kayak paddle lengths are measured in centimeters (cm). The average length of a kayak touring paddle is between 220 and 230 cm (86-90 inches). A racing paddle might be as short as 205 to 210 cm (89-82 inches).

A canoe paddle has to be long enough so the paddler can reach out and place the entire blade area in the water. If the paddle is too long, the entire blade and part of the shaft is in the water. If it's too short, the full surface of the blade is not working the best.

BLADE SIZE AND SHAPE

Wide blades are used when a paddler wants a lot of power—either for a fast start or for quick, powerful maneuvers. Many racers choose a wide paddle blade.

A narrow blade is often the choice of those who like to use a light, but steady stroke. Kayakers or canoers who enjoy a leisure paddle on calm water just need enough power to keep their boats moving forward and in their control.

Paddles with the same shaft length can have different blade shapes and sizes.

Canoers who want a lot of power may have a much wider blade than someone who just wants to cruise quietly. Some blades have square ends, others are rounded. One rounded blade is called the "beaver tail" because its shape is very much like the tail of the animal.

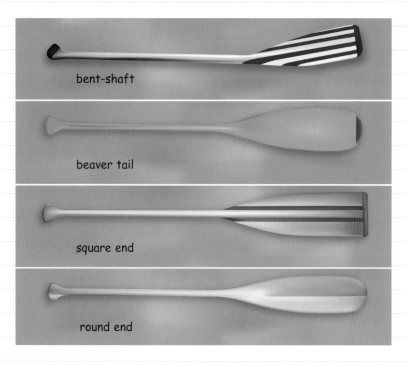

bent-shaft

beaver tail

square end

round end

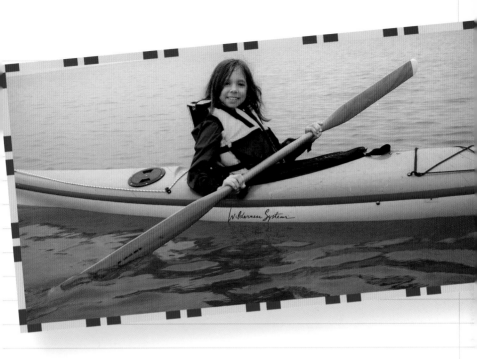

A bent-shaft paddle looks broken because the blade meets the shaft at an angle. This design helps the paddler reach forward farther and faster to paddle more efficiently.

Kayak blades, especially the wider ones, are usually curved from tip to throat, and also from one edge to the other. Some used for racing have a deep curve, almost like a spoon. Others can be almost flat. The most common kayak paddle has a curve that looks very much like the curve of your hand while you are swimming!

A Greenland paddle was designed by kayakers in the country of Greenland. This paddle has very long, narrow blades at the end of a short staff. They are usually made out of one long piece of wood.

PADDLE MATERIAL

Both canoe and kayak paddles can be made of many different materials: wood, aluminum and composite materials such as fiberglass and graphite. Those same materials are also used to make paddle blades. Lightweight, but strong, materials are used for long expeditions, competition and other paddling where every bit of energy is needed.

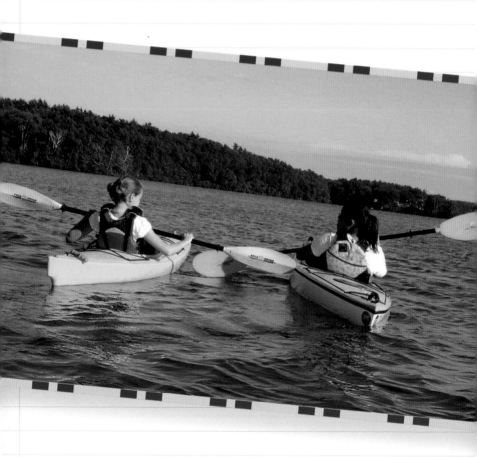

Don't Forget the Spare!

Just like the spare tire carried in a car, a spare paddle is often carried by canoers and kayakers. Sometimes paddles break and you wouldn't want to be out in the middle of a lake without any way of paddling back to shore.

Some paddlers like to have the same quality spare paddle as they have for everyday paddling. Others buy an inexpensive paddle to use in emergencies. A spare canoe paddle is much shorter and can usually be carried somewhere inside the canoe without being in the way. Kayakers usually use the two-piece paddle because it can come apart and be stowed (carried) on the deck of the kayak.

Which Skills Do I Need?

The more you paddle, the more comfortable you will feel in your canoe or kayak. You will learn different ways to steer your boat and different ways to handle many challenging situations. The more you practice, the easier it will be to make the boat feel like it is part of you. That's the sign of a good canoer or kayaker.

The best way to learn how to handle your boat is to learn and practice these three things: proper posture, good paddling strokes and smooth maneuvering techniques.

POSTURE

Good posture when paddling means sitting up straight in the canoe or kayak. Your rear end is right in the center of the seat and your body is facing forward. Your legs are spread apart and your feet and knees are braced against the boat.

If you lean too far to one side, you can upset the balance of the boat. If you slouch over or lean back too far, you won't be able to get all the power and control you need to operate the boat.

As with other sports, you want to build endurance, work on muscle strength and increase stamina. A half hour of hard, consistent paddling is very good exercise. If you are paddling correctly you will be working your arms, shoulders, back, legs and feet to get a well-rounded workout. Even loading and unloading your boat and carrying it to the shoreline are part of the workout.

Paddling for exercise is always a good reason to grab a boat and head to the water. And it will help you keep good posture!

PADDLING STROKES

Pulling your paddle through the water is called a stroke. Different strokes have names that help tell what they do. For example, a forward stroke means you use the paddle to move forward.

Many strokes have the same name when canoeing or kayaking but are done differently because of the difference in the paddle and the design of the boat.

A back stroke is used to move the boat backward. A sweep stroke is used to turn the boat. There are times when you might combine strokes. For example, if you are paddling backward and have to turn the boat slightly to one side, you could use a sweeping backstroke. You can even use a scull stroke to help you move the canoe or kayak sideways through the water!

start scull stroke

finish scull stroke

To get the most out of your stroke, use the muscles in your shoulders and back (called your torso area). Instead of pulling straight back with your arms only, turn your body slightly and let your torso pull, too. You will have a more powerful stroke, be able to paddle for a longer time and get a better workout if you use your upper body instead of just your arms.

Another important part of good paddling technique is to use the foot braces when you paddle. Pushing against them spreads out the power of your stroke. That will help you paddle easier and longer.

For canoeing, the paddle is pulled at a right angle to the surface of the water. Be sure your canoe paddle is the right length so you get the most out of each stroke. The blade should be completely in the water, right up to the throat. If the paddle is too short, part of the blade will be sticking out of the water. If it's too long, the paddle is completely underwater and so is some of the shaft.

Sometimes you will need to switch sides with your paddle to keep your canoe moving straight ahead. This is especially true in a one-person canoe. It takes practice to take your paddle out of the water on one side and then place it back in the water on the other side. If your switch is smooth, your canoe will continue moving in a straight line.

high position

low position

For kayaking, keep your paddle low to the water if you want a relaxing, long stroke. This type of paddling is also good for covering great distances without getting tired. If you want more speed and quick power, use a higher and shorter stroke. Both work best if you keep good posture.

MANEUVERING THE BOAT

Besides basic paddling, you may need to steer your canoe or kayak around rocks or through rapids. A large wave could tip your canoe or capsize your kayak. Practicing what to do in those situations will help you be safe in an emergency.

If your canoe or kayak is upset and you are dumped into the water, you need to know how to get back into it. This can be fun to practice on a hot day, when you like to be in the water anyway.

If your kayak turns over and your spray skirt is snug around you, it can help hold you inside the cockpit. You use your paddle to help you get upright again. This maneuver is called a sweep roll. Be sure to hold your breath when you are underwater practicing this maneuver. You may also want to wear nose plugs!

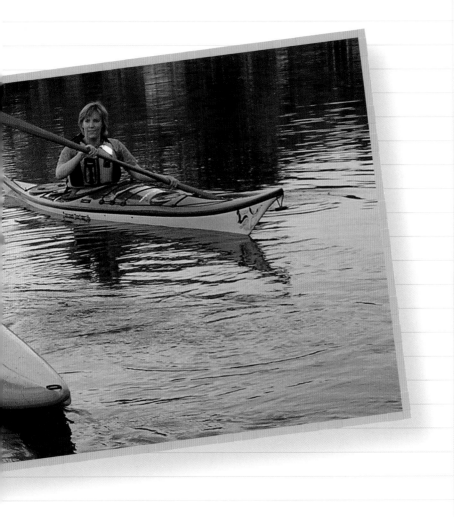

How Do I Prepare for a Trip?

A big part of planning a canoe or kayak trip is to pack as much, or as little, gear as you will need. Then you stow it in places that will keep your boat in balance and easy to maneuver.

There will be days when you paddle around a small bay, or a country lake, or take a short trip down a local river. Other adventures will take you on long journeys in remote areas far from towns and roads. Both types of trips require planning.

USING DRY BAGS

Even a small canoe or kayak can carry a large amount of gear. The trick is to know how to pack it into the boat so all your equipment is dry, convenient to get to when you need it, and packed just right so it doesn't move around or upset the balance of your boat when you are paddling.

A very handy piece of gear is a dry bag, or stuff sack. Dry bags come in a variety of sizes to let you store practically anything: your clothes, a sleeping bag, your tent, camera, cell phone, flashlight, food and cooking gear. If it's something you want to keep from getting wet, put it in a dry bag!

Most dry bags are made of waterproof nylon. Others are made of fabric that is coated with a special plastic that makes the cloth waterproof. Sometimes the cloth-coated bags crack where the bag is repeatedly folded or creased. They don't last as long as the nylon bags. A good dry bag seals so tightly that it locks in the air, keeps water out and continues to protect your gear even if it falls into the water.

Dry bags come in a variety of colors, and some are clear so you can see what's inside.

TRIMMING YOUR BOAT

Placing gear in your canoe or kayak so it doesn't lean to one side or dip in the front or back is called trimming your boat. When you stow your gear in the boat you want to make sure it doesn't shift around. The heaviest pieces should be packed along the centerline of the boat and usually near the middle of the boat (in a canoe) or near the paddler (in a kayak).

Once you start paddling you can tell if your canoe or kayak is trimmed properly. If it tips to one side or the bow seems to be too low or too high in the water, you will have to shift gear around to balance the boat.

There are times when you might make the bow or stern lower or higher by placing gear differently. If the wind is blowing strongly from the front of the boat, you might want to make the bow lower going into the wind by putting slightly more weight toward the front. In a kayak, you might want the stern of the boat lower in the water if seas are pushing you from behind. By carefully packing your boat you can usually make these changes quickly and safely.

Paddlers who take trips for several days need to carry a lot of food. Some paddlers put all the food used to make only their breakfasts in the same color of dry bag. Others put all the food for one day's worth of meals in the same bag. This makes it easier to unload your boat (especially a kayak) when you have lots of bags stuffed inside. If a particular color means it contains food, you don't have to worry about accidentally unloading a bag full of t-shirts when you really want dinner!

Some dry bags serve two purposes. They are often shaped like the bow or stern of the boat, which allows them to be used to store gear in those small areas. And, because they have trapped air inside, they can double as extra flotation.

MAKING A FLOAT PLAN

A float plan is not a list of what you are bringing. It is more like a schedule of where you are going and how long you plan to be gone. You leave it behind so others know when to expect you back or know where to look for you if you don't come back on schedule.

Just telling a friend that you and a buddy are going to canoe down a river and camp on a certain island for the weekend is a simple float plan. A more detailed plan is important when you are going to be gone for a longer time, be farther from home, or perhaps be paddling in a new or remote area.

A good float plan lists everyone in the group. It lists the kinds of boats everyone has and even what color they are. It also tells where you plan to paddle and how long you will stay at each place.

Of course, the plan is no good if you change your mind and go someplace else. If that happens, you should tell someone where you are headed. It could be a ranger, outfitter or other paddlers you meet along the route.

My Paddling Float Plan

Who is paddling:

_____

_____

_____

_____

_____

Start time:

Where are we going:

From_____

_____

To_____

_____

Stop time:

Emergency Phone Numbers:

☐☐☐-☐☐☐-☐☐☐☐

☐☐☐-☐☐☐-☐☐☐☐

My Name:

_____

One important reason for having a float plan is so that someone knows where to find you if you get into trouble. The weather can turn bad and keep you from returning on time. Someone may become ill or get hurt and can't travel. You may be stuck somewhere and run out of food. It will be good to know that someone back home is expecting you and will use the float plan to find you if they have to.

When you are away from home, you can give a copy of your float plan to the harbormaster at the harbor where you launch for your trip. You can give it to a forest or camp ranger, too. You can even tape it to the window of your car so someone can find it if they are looking for you.

Some Questions

Planning ahead will make any trip more fun and enjoyable. Here are a few questions about what to bring on a canoe or kayak trip.

- Will there be beautiful scenery to photograph?

- Should you bring binoculars to watch the wildlife?

- Will your cell phone work in case of an emergency?

- Will you be gone long enough to need extra batteries for your flashlight, camera or cell phone?

- What about a first-aid kit or special medicine for someone in your group?

- Will the weather be changing so you will need special or extra clothing?

- What about having your favorite book to read while you relax in camp?

Where Can I Go?

You may know that the Earth is often called the "water planet" because so much of it is covered by oceans. And even on the continents there are sometimes more lakes than land.

You don't have to go very far, no matter where you live, to find a great place to paddle.

PARKS

City and county parks with lakes or rivers are excellent places to learn how to paddle. As you get more experience you can venture out into your region to find more and more water to explore.

Many state and national parks have water trails for paddling from campsite to campsite on different lakes or down a river running through the park. Some areas have chains of lakes that are all connected to one another by narrow rivers or channels.

Many of these areas have clubs and organizations that offer lessons and special events. They may also have rental boats.

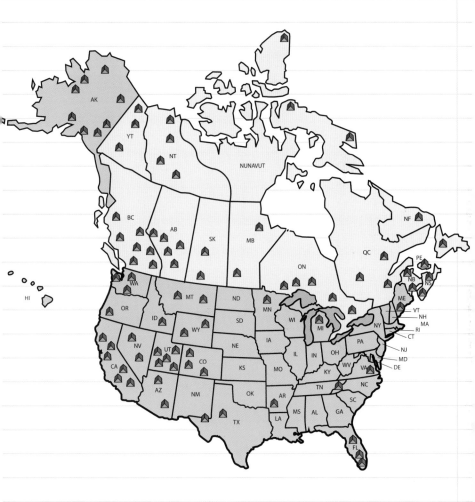

Many states and provinces have national parks, shown on this map with a ⌂ symbol. See the lists on pages 90 and 91 for their name and location.

OCEAN WATERS

The many oceans around the world offer paddlers endless miles (km) of beaches with protective coves and bays or islands to explore.

PACIFIC

The Pacific Northwest region is often called the heart of sea kayaking. It includes the coasts of Washington, Oregon and British Columbia. It has many rapid-flowing rivers for whitewater canoeing and kayaking. The mountain lakes are especially good for canoeing. Ancient paddlers from Alaska and Asia settled here, bringing their kayak traditions with them. Vancouver Island in Canada and Puget Sound in Washington have hundreds of bays to paddle. A big thrill for paddlers in this region is the chance to see a whale or sea lions.

The rugged coast of California has many sandy beaches for launching a kayak, including the Channel Islands National Park.

The Hawaiian Islands and others throughout the South Pacific are great for sea kayaking around islands, coral reefs and atolls in sparkling clear, warm waters.

GULF OF MEXICO

The warm waters of the Gulf of Mexico are very inviting to kayakers. You will find many long stretches of beaches, plus miles (km) of mangrove forests along Florida's southern tip. Fishing from a kayak is very popular in many coastal areas. In protected waters, you will find many places to canoe, including rivers with clear springs.

ATLANTIC

All along the Atlantic Coast are bays, estuaries and
other bodies of water that are perfect for kayaking
and canoeing. Even in the ocean you can find protected
areas where the waves are small and the water is gentle.
Exploring the shoreline in a boat is a wonderful way to
see marine animals.

Maine is especially known as a paddler's playground. It is very popular for kayakers because of its rugged coastline. Acadia National Park is a favorite place for kayakers because of all the islands and tiny bays to explore.

INTERIOR WATERS

Many states and provinces in North America have exciting areas for canoeing and kayaking. Much of the kayaking is whitewater, but any lake you canoe in, you can paddle your kayak, too. Large lakes even have outfitters to help you get the gear you need to enjoy a day or a week of paddling.

EASTERN REGION

In many provinces and states, such as Quebec, Virginia, the Carolinas, Kentucky and Tennessee, you will find fast rivers for whitewater kayaking or canoeing. You will also find many parks and riverways to enjoy all kinds of paddling adventures.

THE GREAT LAKES

The biggest freshwater lakes in the world offer some of the best paddling in all of North America. Many of the northern bays have rocky shorelines with towering cliffs. These lakes can be as cold and raging as the ocean, so you need to be a good paddler!

One example is Isle Royale National Park, which is located in Lake Superior. It has many narrow passages and long bays to explore. You can camp each day in a new spot as you travel around the wilderness island.

The Apostle Islands are also a very popular destination for paddlers on Wisconsin's Lake Superior shoreline. There are several islands you can paddle to that have a network of "sea caves" right on the water. You can paddle into these huge openings and travel through tunnel-like spaces. There are campsites on several islands.

There is also a "water trail" that runs along Minnesota's north shore of Lake Superior, from the town of Two Harbors to the Canadian border. Special campsites and take-out spots at some of Minnesota's prettiest state parks are all part of this new route.

THE MIDWEST

The northernmost part of the Midwest has some of the best "canoe country" in America! There are also many wonderful places in the central part of the United States, some more than 500 miles (800 km) from the nearest ocean where you can enjoy fantastic paddling.

For example, the Boundary Waters Canoe Area Wilderness (BWCAW) and Voyageurs National Park are known for some of the best "canoe country" in the world. There are thousands of lakes and nearly as many miles of rivers joined together to form routes for paddlers—from beginners to old pros. There are tiny islands you can camp on, waterfalls to explore and lakes of all sizes to watch wildlife or catch fish.

The Mississippi River also has areas along the main river channel called sloughs where you can paddle into remote sections that are rich in wildlife. Both canoes and kayaks work well in these areas.

Canoeists find many exciting rivers in this region, too. The St. Croix and Namekogan flow out of Wisconsin. Their waters eventually join with the Mississippi River. You can take day trips or extended journeys down most of these rivers.

Many states have rivers that are so special for paddling that they are designated as wild and scenic rivers. The Current River in central Missouri is a great example.

ALASKA

From glacial bays to chains of lakes, Alaska has it all! Several regions in Alaska offer spectacular kayaking opportunities. There is also expedition-class canoeing in a couple of places.

SOUTHEAST REGION

This area, known as the "panhandle," includes the towns of Ketchikan, Wrangle and others. Coastal kayaking is popular here because of all the remote bays and long fjord-like waterways that cut deep into the Alaska coastline. A favorite kayaking destination is Misty Fjords National Park.

The area around Sitka and Juneau is popular, too. There are even hot springs where you can relax in the warmth of these natural hot pools.

One of the most famous places in this area to paddle is Glacier Bay National Park. It offers paddlers hundreds of remote bays tucked into snow-covered mountains.

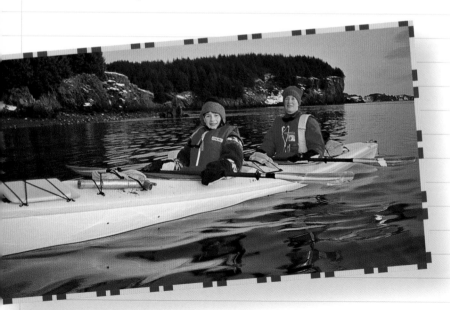

PRINCE WILLIAM SOUND

Between the cities of Whittier on the west and Valdez on the east lies 100 miles (161 km) of ocean with glaciers, remote islands and towering mountains. You can kayak among orca whales and sea otters.

KENAI PENINSULA

Homer and Seward offer many coastal opportunities for kayaking. Kenai Fjords National Park, south of Seward, is renowned for its wildlife viewing and scenery. It's accessible by floatplane from both cities.

KODIAK ISLAND

Just south of the Kenai Peninsula is the island of Kodiak. Its deeply cut bays make it a great place for kayaking. You have a great opportunity to see huge coastal brown bears going after spawning salmon. Shuyak State Park is a popular destination for guided kayaking trips. There you can rent cabins right on the protected bays and enjoy kayaking around the entire island.

OTHER AREAS

There are a couple of really good places to canoe, too. The Swanson River area by Soldotna has miles (km) of river routes through moose country. Wood-Tikchit State Park has a series of remote lakes all connected together. Paddling, fishing and hiking are combined on these trips to make this area one of the best choices for wilderness canoeing.

ALL AROUND THE WORLD

Sea kayaking has become so popular there is only one continent where you can't paddle—the ice continent of Antarctica. The rest of the world, from the largest countries to the smallest ocean islands, have places to paddle. Here are a few of my favorites.

CENTRAL AMERICA

In Mexico, there are two major regions where kayaking is very popular. One area just south of California is Baja. There kayakers can enjoy clear water in a desert environment while watching gray whales gather with their young. Across the country on the Caribbean/Gulf of Mexico side is the state of Yucatan. Here you can paddle the coastline scouting out Mayan ruins and rookeries where beautiful flamingos raise their young.

Costa Rica, Belize and Honduras are among the countries farther south that offer fantastic kayaking in warm, swimming-pool-clear waters. Some of the world's longest coral reefs are here. There are also small, sandy islands that are perfect places to paddle to so you can skin dive with rainbow-colored fish.

NORTHERN EUROPE

In Britain, sea kayaking is called sea canoeing. There are many places to enjoy the rugged scenery of the wild North Atlantic. Bays in Scotland and chains of islands and canals farther south make kayaking and inland canoeing very popular. There are guided kayak tours along the coast of Scandinavia, too, from Norway to Sweden to Finland.

GREECE

Touring companies make it easy for paddlers to visit exotic places. Paddling around the islands of Greece is just one example. The company provides all the paddling gear you need to have a great sea kayaking adventure.

What Else Can I Do?

Paddling can include just the feeling of the breeze as you cruise along a smooth surface, or it can be the sting of mist in your face as you race through a rapids or charge into the waves and wind.

Sometimes your boat is simply a way to enjoy the outdoors in another way. It is a way to get to a place you can't walk to or otherwise experience. Here are a few examples of other activities you can use your boat to enjoy.

EXPLORING

Because canoes and kayaks are so small and can move through the water so quietly, they are excellent boats for exploring. They both can be paddled in very shallow water so they can go where practically no other craft of the same size is able to venture.

Becoming a skilled paddler means learning how to judge different types of waters (rivers, lakes, ponds, channels, reservoirs, special causeways) to make sure they are safe for paddling and exploring.

In some areas of North America, the melting of winter snows means that the backwaters of many rivers overflow, flooding wooded areas along the banks. Sometimes the flooding just covers the low woodlands in a few feet (m) of water making it possible to paddle through trees in the spring that you may be able to hike through later on.

WILDLIFE WATCHING

One of the most popular types of exploring is wildlife viewing and bird watching. The kayak and canoe make it easy to reach remote areas of lakes and rivers and deep into protected bays where wildlife live. Of course being so quiet, it's usually easy to sneak up on animals. You must be very careful to stay far enough away so you don't disturb them or bring danger to yourself. As your balance improves, you will be able to sit still for long periods of time to watch how animals live in the wild.

On oceans it's usually possible to find offshore islands that are homes to many of the sea birds in an area. On lakes, loons are usually found in quiet areas.

Seals and sea lions like to climb up on rocks and warm themselves in the sun. These areas are called "haul outs" and you can usually hear them before you see them. Your kayak is the perfect boat to use as an observation platform from which to enjoy their antics.

Sometimes while paddling along back bays you might see fox or deer or land otters walking along the beach. And don't forget to look up in the sky while paddling, either. You might catch a glimpse of an eagle soaring overhead or terns and other sea birds looking for food.

A special treat when paddling in the ocean is a chance to see a whale. You may see them leap from the water with bodies the size of a school bus!

On lakes and rivers, it is possible to see even more animals than you might see from shore. An hour before sunset you may catch a moose grazing in the reeds. Sometimes deer come down to the water's edge to drink. Raccoons may also be near by.

Shorebirds are always a joy to watch and from a canoe or kayak, you can float through the shallow waters where many of these birds look for food during the day. Sometimes you can surprise a large egret or heron, too. In some parts of North America it's common to see beavers and muskrats swimming across a pond or lake. In warm water, you can add snakes and turtles to the list of animals you might see while paddling.

FISHING & CAMPING

Fishing from a canoe or kayak is like any other kind of fishing, except these are smaller boats. You must bring only the gear you will need. Many paddlers add a fishing rod holder to their boat so they have a place to keep their rod handy.

In a canoe, your tackle box can fit under your seat. In a kayak, even without a spray skirt, you don't have a lot of space to keep your gear handy. One type of kayak that is very popular is called a Sit-On-Top kayak. Instead of sitting down inside the kayak, the paddler of an SOT sits in a seat on top of the boat. There is a special well for the paddler's heel. These boats look like a fat, thick surfboard. You use a regular kayak paddle to move yourself through the water.

Paddling is a great way to find new places to camp, or come ashore and relax. You can plan picnics and other shore snack breaks by carrying a small camp stove and small, soft-sided coolers made especially for packing in a canoe or kayak.

Wherever you paddle, remember: Be safe and have fun!

APPENDIX

As soon as you get home, clean your boat, so it will be ready for your next paddling adventure. If you take care of your equipment, it will last for many years.

BOAT CARE

Wash off any mud, sand, and dry saltwater crystals from the outside of your canoe or kayak. Pay special attention to the rudder, deck and cockpit areas of a kayak. Clean off all weeds so you don't spread them to another area. Be sure to rinse out the inside of your boat, too.

If you practice paddling in a swimming pool, be sure to rinse your boat right after the session. After time, the chemicals in the water may damage the boat.

GEAR STORAGE

Rinse off zippers on life jackets and boots and any-thing else on your boat or gear that snaps, zips or clips together. Be sure everything is completely dry before you put it away.

If you use a two-piece paddle, take it apart and rinse off the ends. Make sure they are dry before you put them back together.

For kayaks, be sure to follow the manufacturer directions to lubricate the moving parts so they continue to work well.

BOAT STORAGE

After a good cleaning, canoes and kayaks can be stored either sitting on one of their sides, on their top or bottom, or hung from straps. It's also important to make sure nothing will fall on the boat if it's stored outside.

If you store your boat on the ground, be sure it doesn't move around. That could accidentally poke a hole in the side.

A canoe stored on a rack or sawhorse should rest on the section of the gunwale where the thwarts are connected. A kayak stored on a rack or sawhorse should rest on the bulkheads.

If you are hanging a boat, make sure the straps are hooked to a strong point on the ceiling or wall. They should wrap around the hull where the thwarts are on the canoe, or where the bulkheads are on the kayak.

You can place a tarp or other covering over the boat. Make sure no water will get in. Some kayakers prefer to use just a cockpit cover to keep out water, dirt and animals.

NATIONAL PARKS

You can learn more information about the U.S. National Parks listed below, plus all the parks in your state, by visiting the National Park Sevice web site: www.nps.gov.

Acadia, ME

Big Bend, TX

Biscayne, FL

Black Canyon of the Gunnison, CO

Channel Islands, CA

Crater Lake, OR

Denali, AK

Dry Tortugas, FL

Everglades, FL

Gates of the Arctic, AK

Glacier, MT

Glacier Bay, AK

Grand Canyon, AZ

Grand Teton, WY

Great Basin, NV

Great Smoky Mtns, NC, TN

Guadalupe Mtns, TX

Hot Springs, AR

Isle Royale, MI

Katmai, AK

Kenai Fjords, AK

King Canyon, CA

Kobuk Valley, AK

Lake Clark, AK

Mount Rainier, WA

North Cascades, WA

Olympic, WA

Redwood, CA

Rocky Mountain, CO

Saguaro, AZ

Sequoia, CA

Shenandoah, VA

Voyageurs, MN

Wrangell Saint Elias, AK

Yellowstone, ID, MT, WY

Yosemite, CA

Zion, UT

You can learn more information about the Canadian National Parks listed below, plus all the parks in your province, by visiting the Parks Canada web site: www.pc.gc.ca.

Aulavik, NT

Auyuittuq, NUN

Banff, AB

Bruce Peninsula, ON

Cape Breton Highlands, NS

Elk Island, AB

Ellesmere Island, NUN

Fathom Five, ON

Forillon, QC

Fundy, NB

Georgian Bay Islands, ON

Glacier, BC

Grasslands, SK

Gros Morne, NF

Gulf Islands, BC

Gwaii Haanas, BC

Ivvavik, YT

Jasper, AB

Kejimkujik, NS

Kluane, YT

Kootenay, BC

Kouchibouguack, NB

La Mauricie, QC

Mingan Archipelago, QC

Mount Revelstoke, BC

Nahanni, NT

Pacific Rim, BC

Point Pelee, ON

Prince Albert, SK

Prince Edward Island, PE

Pukaskwa, ON

Riding Mountain, MB

Saint Lawrence Islands, ON

Sirmilik, NUN

Terra Nova, NF

Tuktut Nogait, NT

Vuntut, YT

Wapusk, MB

Waterton Lakes, AB

Wood Buffalo, AB, NT

Yoho, BC

MORE PADDLING INFORMATION

Here are some ideas for starting your own paddling library. With these books, magazines and videos you'll learn about the history, lore, instruction and adventure of paddling!

BOOKS

Bark Canoes & Skin Boats of North America
by Edwin Tappan Adney
published by U.S. National Museum

Basic Essentials of Canoeing
by Cliff Jacobson
published by Falcon Guides

The Complete Book of Sea Kayaking
by Derek Hutchinson
published by Falcon Guides

The Complete Sea Kayaker's Handbook
by Shelly Johnson
published by Ragged Mountain Press

Nigel Foster's Sea Kayaking
by Nigel Foster
published by The Globe Pequot Press

Fundamentals of Kayak Navigation
by David Burch
published by Pacific Search Press

The Kayak Companion
by Joe Glickman
published by Storey Books

Introduction to Paddling-Basics for Lakes and Rivers
published by American Canoe Association

Qayaq
by David Zimmerly
published by University of Fairbanks Press

MAGAZINES

Canoe & Kayak
www.canoekayak.com

Paddler
www.paddler.com

Rapid
Adventure Kayak
Canoe Root
www.rapidmedia.com

Sea Kayaker
www.seakayakermagazine.com

Wavelength
www.wavelengthmagazine.com

VIDEOS

Performance Sea Kayaking
www.performancevideo.com

University of Sea Kayaking
www.useakayak.org

Seamanship for Kayakers: Getting Started
REI

INDEX

Creative Publishing international
is your Complete Source of How-to Information for the Outdoors

Available Outdoor Titles:

Hunting Books
- Advanced Turkey Hunting
- Advanced Whitetail Hunting
- Black Bear Hunting
- Bowhunters Guide to Accurate Shooting
- Bowhunting Equipment & Skills
- The Complete Guide to Hunting
- Dog Training
- Elk Hunting
- How to Think Like a Survivor
- Hunting Record-Book Bucks
- Kids Gone Campin'
- Mule Deer Hunting
- Muzzleloading
- Outdoor Guide to Using Your GPS
- Pronghorn Hunting
- Waterfowl Hunting
- Whitetail Addicts Manual
- Whitetail Hunting
- Whitetail Techniques & Tactics
- Wild Turkey

Fishing Books
- Advanced Bass Fishing
- The Art of Freshwater Fishing
- Catching Panfish
- The Complete Guide to Freshwater Fishing
- Fishing for Catfish
- Fishing Rivers & Streams
- Fishing Tips & Tricks
- Fishing with Artificial Lures
- Kids Gone Fishin'
- Largemouth Bass

- Live Bait Fishing
- Modern Methods of Ice Fishing
- Northern Pike & Muskie
- Salt Water Fishing Tactics
- Smallmouth Bass
- Successful Walleye Fishing
- Trout
- Ultralight Fishing

Fly Fishing Books
- The Art of Fly Tying – CD ROM
- Complete Photo Guide to Fly Fishing
- Complete Photo Guide to Fly Tying
- Fly-Fishing Equipment & Skills
- Fly Fishing for Beginners
- Fly Fishing for Trout in Streams
- Fly-Tying Techniques & Patterns

Cookbooks
- All-Time Favorite Game Bird Recipes
- America's Favorite Fish Recipes
- America's Favorite Wild Game Recipes
- Backyard Grilling
- Cooking Wild in Kate's Camp
- Dressing & Cooking Wild Game
- The New Cleaning & Cooking Fish
- Preparing Fish & Wild Game
- Recipes from Nature
- The Saltwater Cookbook
- Slow Cookers Go Wild!
- Venison Cookery
- The Wild Butcher
- The Wild Fish Cookbook
- The Wild Game Cookbook

To purchase these or other Creative Publishing international titles, contact your local bookseller, or visit our website at
www.creativepub.com